Tales of the Elves
Based on the Icelandic Folktales of Jón Árnason

Illustrated by Florence Helga Thibault
Adapted by Anna Kristín Ásbjörnsdóttir

Translated by Victoria Cribb

The Origin of the Elves

Once upon a time God came to visit Adam and Eve. They gave him a warm welcome and showed him all they owned. They also showed him their children and he was very pleased with them. He asked Eve if they had any more children apart from the ones she had shown him. No, she said. But it so happened that Eve had not finished washing some of her children, and because she didn't want God to see them, she had hidden them away. God was aware of this and said: 'What is hidden from me shall be hidden from men.' The children now became invisible to other people and lived in hummocks, hills, rocks and mounds. They became the ancestors of the elves or hidden people, while humans are descended from the children that Eve showed to God. Humans can never see elves unless the elves themselves wish it. But the elves can see humans and can make themselves visible when they choose.

Midwife to the Elves

It is said that somewhere east of the mountains a girl once went out late in the evening to bring in the washing. As she was taking down the clothes from the line a strange man appeared. He took her by the hand and asked her to come with him, saying nothing bad would happen to her. Not daring to refuse, the girl went with him. Once they were past the hayfield the man led her down into a mound. Inside was a fine home with all the things you would expect to find in an ordinary house above ground. There she saw a woman lying on the floor, trying in vain to give birth to a baby. The girl laid her hand on the woman and after that all went well and the baby was born.

Afterwards the woman said it was a pity she couldn't repay the girl for her trouble. The girl said it hadn't been much trouble and she didn't expect any reward. But the woman asked her to pass her a glass containing a magic potion. She dipped a feather into the potion and stroked it over the girl's right eye. The girl then said goodbye to the woman, and the man walked her home again. He told her that she would grow up to be a very lucky woman.

The girl often used to say she could see elves. When she saw them taking in their hay, she used to have her own hay taken in too, as she knew that although the weather was sunny, it would soon start to rain. Once when she went into the village she saw the same elf man buying goods from an elf shopkeeper. Without thinking she greeted him, saying: 'Hello, my friend, it's been a long time.' He came over to her at once, put his finger in his mouth and drew it over her eye. After that she never again saw any elves or any of their doings for as long as she lived.

Elf Wind

In the hayfield at the farm of Hörgsland there stands a hummock known as the Elf Mound. In the olden days people used to believe that no one could cut grass on the mound because if they did so a violent storm would arise. So no grass had been cut there for as long as anyone could remember.

There was a farmhand called Jón who didn't believe in such things. One morning the haymakers were out scything the grass around the mound in sunny, windless weather. Then Jón said it wouldn't do any harm to cut some grass on the mound since it grew so lush and thick there. The other farmhands were against this but the farmer wasn't there, so Jón cut the grass some way up the mound.

Afterwards they sat down to whet their scythes in the still weather. But all of a sudden the wind began to gust and all the hay lying on the ground or piled in stacks started to blow away. At that moment the farmer arrived and complained that the hay would be lost in the storm.

The farmhands said it wasn't surprising since Jón had cut grass on the mound although they had warned him against it.

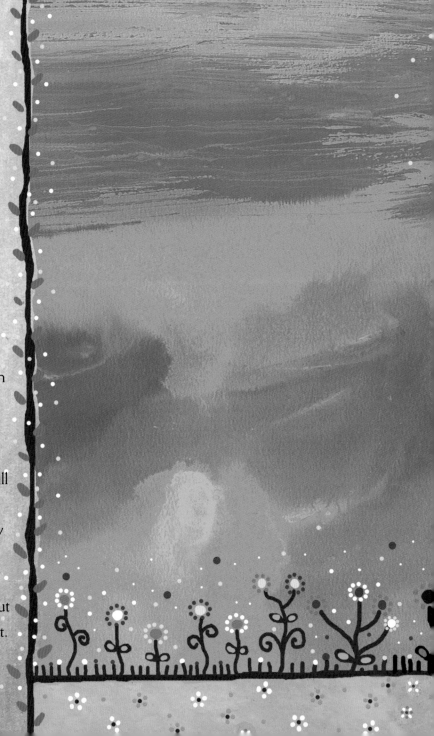

Meanwhile Jón sat there amazed. He thought there was something very fishy going on and he was sure to be blamed for the loss of all the hay. After a short silence he stood up, took his scythe and said aloud so everyone could hear: 'If there's any creature in this mound or anywhere nearby who has raised this great wind, then it must be quite powerful enough to stop it. If it doesn't, I'll cut all the grass on the mound and beat the ground as hard as I can, no matter what happens afterwards.' Jón was now in such a bad temper that he got ready to go and cut the grass. But as he spoke these words the wind began to drop and within a short time all was quiet again. None of the hay was lost and the weather remained calm and sunny for the rest of the day.

Jón later became a farmer at Hamragardar below the Eyjafjöll mountains and told this story himself in 1865.

Payment for Milk

A husband and wife once lived on a farm by Eyjafjord. There was a pantry built on to the farm with a large rock jutting in through the wall.

One evening early in winter the wife went out to the pantry to fetch some food. She noticed a handsome four-pint bowl sitting on the rock, which she had never seen before. She asked the maid about the bowl but the maid had no idea where it came from. The wife poured some fresh milk into the bowl and left it on the rock. Then she removed the pantry key and took it inside the house with her. In the morning the wife went out to the pantry and examined the bowl. It was empty. All winter long the wife poured fresh milk into the bowl every evening and it was always gone next day.

Time now passed until April and the beginning of the Icelandic summer. The night before the first day of summer the wife dreamt that a strange woman came to her and said: 'It was well done of you to give me fresh milk this winter, even though I had done nothing for you. Now you shall receive in return whatever you find when you go into your cowshed in the morning.' With that she vanished.

On the morning of the first day of summer the wife went into the cowshed. There she saw a beautiful heifer that she had never seen before. The wife felt sure the elf woman had given her this heifer in return for the milk. The heifer stayed on the farm from that day on and grew into an excellent cow.

The Elves of Drangey Island

Once upon a time a farmer lived on the farm of Höfdi on the Höfdaströnd coast. It is not known if he had any children with his wife, but he had a foster son whom he loved dearly and who was growing up to be a fine lad. One Christmas Eve, when the boy was in his fourteenth year, the farmhands had to go and fetch some sheep from Drangey Island to feed the household over Christmas. The boy asked his foster father if he could go too. The farmer was reluctant but said at last that if the lads let him go with them, he wouldn't interfere. They set off from land and the trip went well until they had rounded up the sheep and picked out the ones for the feast.

But just before setting off home, the lads pretended they had forgotten some mittens up on the island. The boy offered to run and fetch the mittens, but while he was doing so, they rowed away without him. He watched them go with tears in his eyes. When they were about halfway between the island and the shore a great blizzard blew up so that he lost sight of them and believed their boat must have sunk. He thought he would be left to die on the island from cold and hunger. When he was tired of watching the waves crashing on to the rocks, he decided it was dangerous to stay on the low ground and climbed up the cliffs in search of shelter.

It was freezing hard and the wind was blowing the snow into drifts. He wandered until he came to a hut built to shelter the sheep in snowstorms. Going inside, he gathered up some straw and made himself as cosy as he could. Towards morning he heard a loud noise outside. Next he heard a crowd of people come into the hut, set up tables and lay them with food. Then they began feasting and drinking. If these were kind, generous people they might feel sorry for him, he thought, and even slip him a bite to eat if he showed himself. He leapt hastily to his feet and saw all kinds of food on the tables and people of all ages enjoying the feast. But when they saw the boy they rushed out of the hut, leaving behind all the food and wine. The boy set to eating and had enough food to last him until New Year's Day. He never once left the hut all that time.

Now the story returns to the farmhands who only just made it safely back to land. Nobody at the farm noticed the boy was missing until Christmas morning when they were about to start the singing. The farmer asked if the boy was going to sing with him as usual. Then it was as if the lads who had left the boy behind awoke from a deep sleep. They said they had forgotten all about him because he hadn't been near when they left the island. The farmer was furious and scolded them but nothing else could be done. The blizzard didn't drop until New Year's Day. Then the farmer hurried out to the island but when he couldn't see anyone he was sure his foster son must be dead. Yet he wandered on until he came to the hut. The boy was helping himself to some food when he heard his foster father's voice. Taking a silver cup he went outside to greet the old man and show him the treasure. The old man was overjoyed to see his foster son returned from the dead. After the boy had told him the whole story they went inside the hut but were greeted by thin air because everything had vanished. All they had left was the silver cup the boy had been holding when he heard his foster father's voice.

Queen Bóthildur

One Christmas Eve at the farm of Melar in Hrútafjord there was a knock at the door. Outside stood a richly dressed woman, asking for shelter. The sheriff who lived at Melar in those days said that she could stay. When people asked her name she said she was called Bóthildur, but she wouldn't say where she had come from or where she had grown up. She stayed the night, remaining alone at home while the rest of the household went to midnight mass. When the people came home in the morning they had never seen the house so beautifully swept and cleaned or everything so well prepared. The sheriff invited her to stay longer, so she became his housekeeper and proved good at her job. Next Christmas Eve all the people went to church except Bóthildur. When they came home in the morning they saw that she was very sad and her eyes were red with weeping, something that had never happened before.

On the third Christmas night she again stayed alone at home. But this time the sheriff's shepherd boy Gudmundur swore he would find out what she got up to, so he pretended to fall ill after everyone had set off for church and turned back home again. He had a magic stone that made him invisible, and taking this in his hand he went into the living room. There he saw her dressing herself in the finest clothes he had ever seen. Then she took a green cloth out of a chest and went outside.

Gudmundur followed her until they came to a lake. She spread the cloth on the water and stepped on top of it. Gudmundur managed to climb on to a corner of the cloth before it started to sink. It seemed to him as if they were passing through smoke as they sank down into the earth until at last they came to a beautiful grassy plain. He saw the high towers of a fair city before him and tallest of all was the church in the middle. Bóthildur walked to the city where she was greeted with joy. A man whom Gudmundur took to be the most important person there, since everyone else obeyed him, embraced her and kissed her as if she was his wife, and three children greeted her as if she was their mother. Everyone was happy when they saw Bóthildur and welcomed her. Next they went to church where they held mass as Christians do. Bóthildur's children ran around between the pews, playing with three golden rings. The youngest lost his ring and couldn't find it because Gudmundur had taken it and put it in his pocket.

After church people sat down to a banquet, with Bóthildur seated on a throne beside her husband. They ate well and drank well until dawn when Bóthildur stood up and said it was time for her to leave. Everyone was sad at this, especially her husband.

She said goodbye to them all but her husband walked with her, bewailing the fact that they couldn't be together and that this was the last time they would ever meet. They then parted from each other with great sorrow.

She stepped back on to the cloth, with Gudmundur beside her, and returned the same way as before. Afterwards she walked home to Melar and took off her finery. Then she started her chores and everything was ready as usual by the time the party came home from church.

Gudmundur came home too and the sheriff asked where he had been. He said he had been exploring the settlements down below. The sheriff asked him why. Gudmundur said he had been following the sheriff's housekeeper. He then told the whole story while Bóthildur listened. In the end she asked if he could show any proof that he was telling the truth. He drew out the ring and showed it to her. Bóthildur was glad and said: 'What you have said is true, and I owe you a great reward. I was once a queen in Elf Land until a witch laid a spell on me that I should leave and live with humans and never be allowed home to Elf Land except on Christmas night. I would not be released from the spell until some human was bold enough to go down there with me. Now you have released me from the spell and you shall be richly rewarded.' Then, after saying goodbye to the sheriff and all his household, she vanished. The following night she came to Gudmundur in a dream and gave him a huge pile of coins and many jewels which he found on his pillow when he woke up. Later he bought himself a farm, got married and was the luckiest man alive.

Fostered by the Elves

A pauper boy called Jón once lived on a farm south of the moors. He was about six years old when this story begins. He was cared for by an old woman and they both slept in the cowshed where their food was brought out to them. The old woman noticed that the boy often held out some of his food and drink. When she asked him why, he answered that there was a woman in one of the stalls who was holding out her hand to him. The old woman said nothing but began to do the same herself. So the winter passed. One night in spring the old woman dreamt that a woman came to her and thanked her kindly on behalf of herself and her family but said she couldn't repay them as she should: 'But as I know you love the boy no less than yourself I will offer to take him home with me where my husband, who is a priest in this parish, will teach him to be a priest and give him the same schooling as our own children.' The old woman agreed to this in her dream. When she woke up in the morning the boy was gone. She thought this strange but then remembered the dream. People often talked about his disappearance but quickly changed the subject. The old woman was never happy from this time on.